LET'S WORK IT OUT™

How to deal with COMPETITIVENESS

Rachel Lynette

PowerKiDS press™

New York

Published in 2009 by The Rosen Publishing Group, Inc.
29 East 21st Street, New York, NY 10010

Copyright © 2009 by The Rosen Publishing Group, Inc.

First Edition

Editor: Joanne Randolph
Book Design: Kate Laczynski
Photo Researcher: Jessica Gerweck

Photo Credits: Cover, p. 1 © Bob Thomas/Getty Images; pp. 4, 12, 14 Shutterstock.com; p. 6 © Elyse Lewin/Getty Images; p. 8 © Alistair Berg/Getty Images; p. 10 © Photo and Co./Getty Images; p. 16 © Ben Weaver/Getty Images; p. 18 © David Madison/Getty Images; p. 20 © Chris Cole/Getty Images.

Library of Congress Cataloging-in-Publication Data

Lynette, Rachel.
  How to deal with competitiveness / Rachel Lynette. — 1st ed.
      p. cm. — (Let's work it out)
  Includes index.
  ISBN 978-1-4042-4521-1 (library binding)
  1. Competition (Psychology)—Juvenile literature. I. Title.
  BF637.C47L96 2009
  302'.14—dc22
                                        2008009697

Manufactured in the United States of America

Contents

When we play games, such as checkers or chess, we are competing. Competing can be fun, as long as no one cares too much about winning.

What Is Competitiveness?

Emily and Maria were painting. "My picture is better than yours," said Emily. "I used more colors. Yours does not look real."

Why do you think Emily said those things to Maria? How do you think it made Maria feel? Competitiveness means trying to win or trying to be better than other people. People are competitive when they play a game. People are also competitive when they **compare** themselves to other people. When Emily compared her picture to Maria's, she was being competitive. Can you think of a time when you felt competitive?

Sometimes people compete to show that they are good at something. This girl is competing in her school spelling bee.

Why Are People Competitive?

People are often competitive when they are playing a sport or a game. People are also competitive when they enter a **contest**, like a science fair. Most people want to win.

Sometimes people are competitive because they feel **insecure**. Katie was worried that she was not good at spelling. When she got more words right than the kids around her, Katie felt better.

Another reason someone might feel competitive is to gain another person's **approval**. Tim wanted to be the best player on his soccer team because he wanted his father to be proud of him.

Competing is good when everyone is having fun, like these children are. They want to win, but they will not be upset if they lose.

Good Competition

Erin and Michael each decided to run for class president. They both made posters and gave good speeches. When the class voted, Erin won. Michael felt a little sad, but he also felt proud of himself for trying. He made sure to **congratulate** Erin on her win.

Competition can be a good thing. When people want to win, they may try harder and play better. However, winning is not the most important thing. Competition is good only when people remember that having fun, learning new things, and playing fair are more important than winning.

When competing is not fun, it is not a good competition anymore. Instead of feeling bad about losing, try to think of ways to do better next time.

Bad Competition

Competition is bad when winning becomes the most important thing. When this happens, people often get upset. They may get angry and say mean things. They may quit or try to win by cheating, or tricking people. Sometimes people get into fights over a game. Then the game is not fun for anyone.

Competition is also bad when a person compares himself to other people. There will always be people who are better and worse at things than you are. Instead of comparing yourself to others, work on improving your own skills. Be proud of yourself for doing your best!

Steven's brother always beat him when they raced. Steven did not feel bad, though, because he knew that he was better at other things.

Competing with Brothers and Sisters

Kate and Jenny are twins. They both entered an art contest at school. Kate won! Jenny felt sad and **jealous**.

It can be hard when your brother or sister, or sibling, is better at something than you are. It can help to remember that everyone has different skills. Think about what you do well. You might want to find a new activity or sport that your sibling does not do.

If you are the one who did well, try to be **sensitive** to your sibling's feelings. What could you say to make your sibling feel better?

Try to use competition in school to push you to do your best. You do not need to have all the answers, as long as you are trying.

14

Competing in School

Children often compete in school. Sometimes teachers put up star charts or give **rewards** to children who do well. If you are struggling in school, it can be hard to see your classmates doing better than you are.

Brad's teacher gave students gold stars for passing math **tests**. Most of the other children had a lot of stars. Brad did not have any. Brad decided to study hard and do his best. The next day he passed the test. Brad got a star! Even though it was only one star, Brad was proud of himself. Soon he had more stars!

Staying positive and cheering on teammates will make everyone have more fun. Working together is more important than winning.

Competing in Sports

Do you play on a team? Playing team sports can be lots of fun! Just remember that you are playing to learn new skills and to make friends. It is fun to win, but it is not the most important thing.

When you play on a team, be sure you say only positive things, even if your team is losing. It is not okay to make a person feel bad because she is not a good player. If you think about saying something **negative**, stop yourself. Instead, remember that everyone is trying their best.

Passing the ball to others is an important part of being a good team player. Not everyone will be as good as you are, but they are part of the team.

18

Being a Good Team Player

Even though Kim is the best player on her team, she makes sure to pass the ball to her teammates. When one of her teammates makes a mistake, Kim always says, "Good try!" Kim does not get upset, even when her team is losing. Kim knows how to be a good team player.

When you play on a team, remember that everyone is an important part of the team. Good team players **cooperate** with their teammates. They **encourage** them and treat them with respect. Good team players always follow the rules and play fair. Are you a good team player?

Whether you win or lose, you should congratulate the other team for playing a good game. Remember, sports are supposed to be fun!

Being a Good Sport

What does it mean to be a good sport? A good sport knows how to win. Good sports do not brag or say negative things about the losing team. Instead, they tell the other team that they played a good game or that they were hard to beat.

Good sports also know how to lose. Good sports remember that the fun is in playing the game. They do not get upset or angry when their team is losing. They do not quit. Good sports say positive things about their teammates and congratulate the winning team. How else can you be a good sport?

Everybody Wins

How can you tell if a competition that you are a part of is good or bad? Think about how you feel. Are you having fun? Are the people around you happy? If everyone is having fun, then the competition is a good one!

What if people are not having fun? If people are upset, it might be a good idea to think about what is going wrong. What can you do to make things better?

When people are good team players and good sports, competition is fun. When competition is fun, everybody wins!

Glossary

approval (uh-PROO-vul) The act of thinking well of someone or something.

compare (kum-PER) To see how two or more things are alike or unlike.

congratulate (kun-GRA-joo-layt) To tell someone one is proud of him or her.

contest (KON-test) A match or game between two or more sides to see who will win.

cooperate (koh-AH-puh-rayt) To be happy to work with others.

encourage (in-KUR-ij) To give hope, cheer, or certainty.

insecure (in-seh-KYUR) Not feeling sure about something, shy or not confident.

jealous (JEH-lus) Wanting what someone else has.

negative (NEH-guh-tiv) Looking at the bad, or down, side of things.

rewards (rih-WORDZ) Things given to people who have done a good job.

sensitive (SEN-sih-tiv) Aware of what is going on.

tests (TESTS) Things that check how well people know a topic.

Index

Web Sites

Due to the changing nature of Internet links, PowerKids Press has developed an online list of Web sites related to the subject of this book. This site is updated regularly. Please use this link to access the list:

www.powerkidslinks.com/lwio/compet/